Lay Counseling Series

Psychologists and Theologians,
Can They Integrate?

Jerry E. McKeehan

LAY COUNSELING SERIES

This book is written to provide information and motivation to readers. Its purpose is not to render any type of psychological, legal, or professional advice of any kind. The content is the sole opinion and expression of the author, and not necessarily that of the publisher.

Copyright © 2019 by Jerry E. McKeehan

All rights reserved. No part of this book may be reproduced, transmitted, or distributed in any form by any means, including, but not limited to, recording, photocopying, or taking screenshots of parts of the book, without prior written permission from the author or the publisher. Brief quotations for noncommercial purposes, such as book reviews, permitted by Fair Use of the U.S. Copyright Law, are allowed without written permissions, as long as such quotations do not cause damage to the book's commercial value. For permissions, write to the publisher, whose address is stated below.

Printed in the United States of America.

ISBN   978-1-949746-97-6   (Paperback)
ISBN   978-1-949746-98-3   (Digital)

Lettra Press books may be ordered through booksellers or by contacting:

Lettra Press LLC
18229 E 52nd Ave.
Denver City, CO 80249
1 303 586 1431 | info@lettrapress.com
www.lettrapress.com

MSG
Scripture quotations marked MSG are taken from The Message. Copyright © 1993, 1994, 1995, 1996, 2000, 2001, 2002, 2003 by Eugene H. Peterson. Used by permission of NavPress Publishing Group. Website.

ESV
Unless otherwise indicated, all scripture quotations are from *The Holy Bible, English Standard Version® (ESV®)*. Copyright ©2001 by Crossway Bibles, a division of Good News Publishers. Used by permission. All rights reserved.

NASB
Scripture quotations marked NASB are taken from the *New American Standard Bible®*, Copyright © 1960, 1962, 1963, 1968, 1971, 1972, 1973, 1975, 1977, 1995 by The Lockman Foundation. Used by permission.

NRSV
Scripture quotations marked NRSV are taken from the *New Revised Standard Version of the Bible*, Copyright © 1989, by the Division of Christian Education of the National Council of the Churches of Christ in the United States of America. Used by permission. All rights reserved.
Website

HCSB
Scripture quotations marked HCSB are from the Holman Christian Standard Bible®. HCSB®. Copyright ©1999, 2000, 2002, 2003 by Holman Bible Publishers. Used by permission. Holman Christian Standard Bible®, Holman CSB®, and HCSB® are federally registered trademarks of Holman Bible Publishers

NKJV
Scripture quotations marked NKJV are taken from the New King James Version. Copyright © 1982 by Thomas Nelson, Inc. Used by permission. All rights reserved.

NLT
Scripture quotations marked NLT are taken from the *Holy Bible, New Living Translation*, copyright © 1996, 2004, 2007. Used by permission of Tyndale House Publishers, Inc. Carol Stream, Illinois 60188. All rights reserved. Website

NCV
Scripture quotations marked "NCV" are taken from the New Century Version, Copyright © 1987, 1988, 1991 by Word Publishing, a division of Thomas Nelson, Inc. Used by permission. All rights reserved.

Psychologists and Theologians, can they integrate?

Counseling Definition

Counseling (people helpers) involves the establishment of a time-limited relationship that is structured to provide comfort for troubled persons by enhancing their awareness of *God's grace* and *faithful presence* and thereby increasing their ability to live their lives more fully in the light of these realizations. (1)

> Dr. Gary Collins

Dr. John White says it well: "People who want to help people need two Things": First, a profound understanding of the deepest needs of the human heart. Second, an ongoing experience of having their own needs met. (2)

> Putting the Soul Back into Psychology

Paul Tournier, in his book "Secrets", puts it this way:

> "The most powerful means of getting to know ourselves is to allow ourselves to be examined by God and to listen to what he has to say to us, for he knows us better than we know ourselves. He knows all our secrets. Nothing escapes him" (3)

> Paul Tournier, Secrets,

Introduction

Is a pastor without psychological training qualified to counsel his flock, or must he limit himself to spiritual counseling and refer the more difficult cases to professionals?

Many Bible school graduates think they have to get a doctorate in psychology at a state university so they can become a counselor. They think they have to combine psychological training with their Bible school knowledge for maximum effectiveness. But psychologists and theologians dispute the extent to which psychological studies can successfully integrate with the Bible.

Personally, I am wary about attempts at integration. I find no biblical support to distinguish a spiritual problem from a psychological one.

<u>Kirwan, William T. Biblical Concepts for Christian Counseling says</u>:

"Like any science, psychology merely observes. By definition, it cannot make a statement about the meaning of life, nor can it supply us with values, morals, goals, orproper motivations. Yet human beings are vitally interested in these matters.

Psychologists can clinically observe basic human nature, they can study brain waves in the laboratory, but they cannot speak with authority about the philosophical implications of their observations. Of course, psychologists as individuals hold all sorts of philosophical ideas.

Regrettably, philosophical statements made by leaders in psychiatry and psychology have caused a large number of Christians to be skeptical of the entire scientific enterprise. For example, Freud attributed belief in God to human wishes arid fears. Rogers renounced his earlier Christian beliefs. Skinner has said that human beings are biologically determined.

Such statements, however, do not mean that we must discard all the findings of those schools which Freud, Rogers, and Skinner so ably represent. We simply need to recognize when they are speaking as philosophers and when they are speaking as psychologists.

At root, man's psychological problems, unless due to physical or chemical causes, are spiritual— and where could we find a better analysis of man's need along with a supernatural remedy than in the Scriptures?" (4)

The Solution

Peter writes that our Lord's divine power has granted us *"everything pertaining to life and godliness, through the true knowledge of Him who called us by His own glory and excellence"* (2 Peter 1:3).

Paul writes, *"For in Him all the fulness of Deity dwells in bodily form, and in Him you have been made complete, and He is the head over all rule and authority"* (Colossians 2:9-10). That leaves little room for using the techniques of secular psychology to help Christians achieve emotional and spiritual wholeness. I admit, however, that God has often used Christian counselors who have built on the theories of secular psychology. God's Word is always effective regardless of the context in which it is believed and obeyed. And in some instances psychological studies have hit upon biblical truths. So psychology may have some value in helping us understand man's predicament from a different perspective.

Lawrence Crabb, in his book Effective Biblical Counseling, advocates that we "spoil the Egyptians"— we should use the insights, principles, and techniques of psychology that are consistent with Scripture to help us become more effective.

I appreciate his desire to test the presuppositions of secular theories so that we would accept only what is biblical. But even then, I suspect that if we'd take the time to analyze the text, we would find that such psychological insights are already in the Scriptures. (5)

A biblical approach. It's unfortunate that the expression "biblical counseling" has a negative connotation. Some think it means that the antidote to every problem is just information, and the relationship between the counselor and the counselee is therefore mechanistic and impersonal. A thoroughly biblical approach rejects such a simplistic notion.

Paul stressed the personal dimension in exhortation and encouragement. He fathered those who needed discipline and mothered those who needed tender care (1 Thessalonians 2:7).

A reflective knowledge of the Scriptures along with a compassionate heart can, under the guidance of the Spirit, be used to uncover the root cause of problems that elude a purely psychological approach.

In our fallen world, there is a battle for our affection and attention, for our love and loyalty. In this battle, Satan says, "The world is ugly so God must be ugly too. Live an ugly life." Christ says something very different to us: "Life in a fallen world is bad and ugly. But God is good and beautiful — he alone is good and he is good all the time. Live a beautiful life for his beautiful glory."

The battle for our minds and hearts is won or lost according to our image of God. Since we reflect what we revel in and become like what we worship, we must know God in all his majesty and beauty if we are to become like him.

When life's struggles hit, we don't simply help one another with solutions to problems. Instead, we help one another with soul-u-tions (change at the heart level) by helping one another to grasp who God is and encouraging one another to respond like Christ.

Biblical counselors know God. They enlighten their spiritual friends to grasp the holy love of God. They expose Satan's deceitful veiling of God's glory and grace that invades their spiritual friends' lives. They teach that God is good even when life is bad. He is not only the author of our story, God is the protagonist in the story — the good guy, our loving conqueror.

Jared Wilson says it well in Gospel Wakefulness: "The Bible may be an epic love story, but we are not the protagonists in it. The Bible's story is about God. He is its chief character. He is the hero." (6)

A BASIC UNDERSTANDING OF FIVE LIFE NEEDS

I have come to believe that all people, have five core needs:

- Security
- Identity
- Belonging
- Purpose
- Competence

These are the five basic life questions that need an answer:

1. "Who can I trust?" (the question of security)
2. "Who am I?" (the question of identity)

3. "Who wants me?" (the question of belonging)
4. "Why am I alive?" (the question of purpose)
5. "What do I do well?" (the question of competence)

A BASIC UNDERSTANDING OF FIVE LIFE SKILLS

Now with the five life questions above, we have five basic life skills that correspond with the same core needs: These life skills will need to be practiced for the rest of one's life.

1. "How to forgive?" (the life skill of security)
2. "How to change?" (the life skill of identity)
3. "How to Choose/Make/Keep Friends?" (the life skill of belonging)
4. "How to Love God and Others?" (the life skill of purpose)
5. "How to Make Decisions?" (the life skill of competence)

Again, these life skills will need to be practiced for the rest of one's life.

The chart looks like this:

Need No.	Core Need	Life Question	Life Skill
1	Security	Who can I trust?	How to Forgive
2	Identity	Who am I?	How to Change
3	Belonging	Who wants me?	How to Choose/Make/Keep Friends
4	Purpose	Why am I alive?	How to Love God and Others
5	Competence	What do I do well?	How to Make Decisions

A BASIC UNDERSTANDING OF PROBLEM DEVELOPMENT

We tend to minister to symptoms, healing people "slightly" while leaving the roots of the problem untouched.

Jeremiah 8:11 reads:

> "[11] They have treated superficially the brokenness of My dear[a] people, claiming, 'Peace, peace,' when there is no peace."

Jeremiah 8:22 reads:

> Is there no balm in Gilead? Is there no physician there? So why has the healing of my dear[c] people not come about?"

Ezekiel 18:1-20 reads: (Message)

> "...[20]The soul that sins is the soul that dies. The child does not share the guilt of the parent, nor the parent the guilt of the child. If you live upright and well, you get the credit; if you live a wicked life, you're guilty as charged."

"Ministers seemed to me like gardeners continually lopping off weeds which just as persistently re-grew from the roots. *Most* seem not to comprehend the whole job, to lay the ax to the root. Roots lie hidden, beneath the surface." (7) Agnes Sanford

1. Beneath the symptoms (hidden by suppression and repression) are feelings of anger, guilt, anxiety, fear, and tormented feelings which find their roots in unforgiveness, bitterness, records of wrongs, and unresolved conflict in the inner man (Matthew 18:21-35).

2. Beneath the feelings are hurts caused by significant people in our lives and our sinful reactions to those hurts.

3. Yet beneath the hurts are unmet needs, needs that only God can ultimately meet.

a). God's goal in our hurt is to draw us to Himself.

b). All our difficulties, whether the result of our own sin or not, are custom designed by God to teach us how to apply His grace and forgiveness.

See illustration of problem development – Appendix A.

WHY DOES THIS CONFLICT EXIST IN THE LIFE OF A BELIEVER?

The spirit and/or nature is new, but the mind needs to come under the authority of the new spirit (as does the body).

a). Renewing of the mind (Romans 12:1-2)

"I therefore urge you, brothers, in view of God's mercies, to offer your bodies as living sacrifices that are holy and pleasing to God, for this is the reasonable way for you to worship.[a] ² Do not be conformed to this world, but continuously be transformed by the renewing of your minds so that you may be able to determine what God's will is—what is proper,[b] pleasing, and perfect" (Romans 12:1-2 ISV)

---

b). 2 Corinthians 10:5 "captivity" means to take by the spear.

The soul needs healing, the giving and receiving of grace, forgiveness, and re-training (Matthew 11:28; Psalm 23:3).

c). Our Sin Nature: We fail to put the ax to the root of the tree, the power of the cross to put to death the old sin nature (Colossians 3:5,9,12).

d). The Holy Spirit is not making us better, but bringing us into fullness of death (Romans 12:1; Romans 6:3-11).

e). We fail to repent fully at conversion (Numbers 33:55).

Lack of teaching and/or obedience regarding:

a). <u>The Importance of the Bible</u>

- The Bible is the inspired Word of God and has the right to command my beliefs, actions and virtue.

"All Scripture is given by inspiration of God, and is profitable for **doctrine**, for **reproof**, for **correction**, for **instruction** in righteousness, that the man of God may be complete, thoroughly equipped for every good work" (2 Tim. 3:16-17).

- Inspiration—God has taken the inactive to make himself known
- Doctrine—what's right
- Reproof—what's not right
- Correction—how to get right
- Instruction—how to stay right

The Bible gets down to where people, not angels, live. After all, a man sinking in the depths of sin does not ask: "Is there a God?" His plea is: "Tell me how one who deserves the judgment of death can find a God of forgiveness!" The power of the Word is its ability to answer such questions.

Our Understanding about Salvation

Three ideas are essential to the concept:

- First, Salvation is a process, not an event or a moment.
- Second, Life in the kingdom of God is available right now, not merely after bodily death. God partners with

an individual who not only accepts God's offer but continues to "work out your salvation with fear and trembling" (Phil. 2:12)
- Third, we do not have a product to push but a person to reveal. Jesus Christ!

Our New identity in Christ (Justification)

I am significant because of my position as a child of God.

> "However, to all who received him, those believing in his name, he gave authority to become God's children" John 1:12 (ISV)

Justification is the forgiveness of sins and the regeneration of the soul, along with an attendant assurance of everlasting life in the presence of God. Justification is a new beginning for a relationship that has been broken, and it is made right by forgiveness, but that's just the doorway into the resumption of relationship.

The Kingdom of God, and ongoing salvation (Sanctification)

Let's read what Jesus said in John 17:16-17:

> "They are not of the world, even as I am not of it," and this is before His request: "Sanctify them by the truth; your word is truth" (John 17:16-17).

Sanctification is itself a process by which the inner person of an individual comes to resemble Christ's inner person. The end goal of sanctification is Christlikeness. It is, simply put, 'the process of becoming holy'.

The Role of Grace

In the New Testament, "grace" (156 times) takes on a special redemptive sense in which God makes available his favor on behalf of sinners, who actually do not deserve it.

Grace, within the context of the Gospel, is the free gift of a merciful God. Though mankind was made to glorify our Creator and to enjoy his fellowship, we have all turned to our own way, scorning his love, blaspheming his name, and we have brought on ourselves the just sentence of death. Humankind deserves nothing but hell.

The Filling of the Holy Spirit (Ephesians 5:18)

Let's start: What is clear about the Holy Spirit?

- The Holy Spirit is a person.

a) He is a counselor (John 14:26)
b) He has a mind, as when "He teaches all things" (John 14:26)
c) He has emotions, as when He "grieves" (Ephesians 4:30)
d) He has a will, as when He "forbids" (Acts 16:6-7)
e) "You will know Him, for He dwells with you, and will be in you" (John 14:17)

- The Holy Spirit is God.

a) "...for what *reason* has Satan filled your heart, *that* you **lied to the Holy Spirit** and kept back for yourself *some* of the proceeds of the piece of land? ⁴ *When it* remained to you, did it not remain *yours*? And *when it*[g] was sold, was it at your disposal? How *is it* that you have contrived this deed in your heart? You have not **lied** to people, **but** (lied) **to God!**" (Acts 5:4)

- When one receives Christ the Holy Spirit enters one's life (1 Corinthians 12:13).
- The Holy Spirit does not come in measure (John 3:34)
- We have the same Holy Spirit in us that dwelt in our Lord Jesus.
- We do not need more of the Holy Spirit. The Holy Spirit wants more of us!

The Holy Spirit has a threefold ministry (8)

- The Holy Spirit works in us:

a) **Before** *conversion*—when he illuminates the minds of seekers (1 Corinthians 12:3) and convicts them of their sin and need of a savior (John 16:8).
b) **At** *conversion*—when he regenerates (John 3:5-6) and then indwells the lives of believers (Romans 8:9-10; 1 Corinthians 3:16; 2 Corinthians 1:22), and finally seals them as purchased possessions (Ephesians 1:13).
c) **After** *conversion*—when he sanctifies disciples (1 Thessalonians 4:7-8; 1 Corinthians 6:19-20), guides them (John 16:13), helps them to pray (Romans 8:26-27), strengthens them (Ephesians 3:16), brings forth his fruit (Galations 3:22-23). And equips them for service through his gifts (1 Corinthians 12:4-11). (8

"Stop getting[a] drunk with wine, which leads to wild living, but KEEP on being filled with the Spirit" Ephesians 5:18 (ISV)

Did the disciples receive the Holy Spirit before Pentecost?

Let's look at John 20:22 (ISV) Jesus said:

"**21** Jesus told them again, "Peace be with you. Just as the Father has sent me, so I am sending you." **22** When he had said this, he breathed on them and told them, "Receive the Holy Spirit.

Some fine men of God have told us this was Jesus giving a promise of the future Pentecost.

Here is the problem, the word "receive" is NOT in the promise form. The word "receive" in Greek is in the command form. The word "receive" is in the "Second Aorist Imperative". It means: "When spoken by one in authority the command is obeyed immediately!" I believe

I have come to believe the command to be filled with the Holy Spirit is what happened at Pentecost. The words used in Acts 2:4: "All of them were filled with the Holy Spirit..." Did the Baptism in the Holy Spirit occur at Pentecost? Yes! Does this mean one is filled or baptized in the Holy Spirit at conversion? Nope. If being filled with the Holy Spirit was automatic? There would be no need for a command to KEEP be filled with the Holy Spirit!

Lack of Repentance:

Repentance is a discovery of the evil of sin, a mourning that we have committed it, a resolution to forsake it. It is, in fact, a change of mind of a very deep and practical character, which makes the man love what once he hated, and hate what once he loved.

J. I. Packer writes: (Truly God's Grace)

Repentance means turning from as much as you know of your sin to give as much as you know of yourself to as much as you know of your God, and as our knowledge grows at these three points so our practice of repentance has to be enlarged.

John Piper writes:

Repenting means experiencing a change of mind that now sees God as true and beautiful and worthy of all our praise and all our obedience. (9)

For further reflection, see John Piper's article titled "Thoughts on Jesus' Demand to Repent."

Forgiveness (Giving and Receiving)

- This probably is our most important DIVEDEND (bonus) we receive from Christ.
- Forgiveness is releasing another from any claims you might have to revenge or restitution.

David Seamonds, writes in his book <u>Healing for Damaged Emotions</u>:

"Two major causes of emotional problems...

- First, failure to receive forgiveness.
- Second, failure to give forgiveness." (10)

Worship (Individual and Corporate)

- I honor God in the way he deserves my worship! I worship God for who He is and what He has done for me... for the Purpose of Godliness (Psalm 95:1-7).
- The truth is that worship, like all devotion, is *for God's sake*. We do not worship for what we can get out of it, but for what God's kingdom can get out of it.

Why do we worship, pray, study, etc.—to enhance our own standing before God and others, or to enhance God's standing in the world?

I have made it a point to conduct a survey in each of the churches I've served and attended in the past forty years, asking the members to indicate why they come to church. In every case, the answers have varied widely, but they all share a common idea. First, let's look at the answers which are most often given, and then talk about the topic.

To the question, "Why do you come to church?" the most frequently given answers are:

- To feel God's presence;
- To learn more about God;
- To be with my Christian friends;
- To give my children a Christian environment;
- To gain the strength to face life weekly;
- To keep myself morally pure;
- For the preaching;
- For the music;
- For the Bible study;
- It's just something I've always done;
- It makes me feel good.

Rarely have I found answers which are not included in the above. What do these responses say about our devotion? Obviously, that for a great number of Christians, devoutness is a self-serving enterprise! It is primarily designed to enhance one's standing before God and men. It is designed for the purpose of receiving, not giving!

Let's face it, most people go to church much in the same way as they go to a mechanic when their car is broken, or to a physician when they are ill. That is, they go in order to have their needs cared for. As someone has said, the Church is a "covenant of personal concerns, not a covenant of servants who have united to transform the world."

Perhaps we should inject here that there's nothing wrong with embracing God out of personal need. After all, where else can a person go when he is broken? The Bible does picture Jesus as the Great Physician, and he *did* say, "Come unto me, all of you who are heavy laden, and I will give you rest" (Matt. 11:28).

There is nothing wrong with turning to God out of personal concern; but here is where the disturbing part comes in: *The church is not God! It is not a hospital where one goes to be healed! The church is a fellowship of persons who have already been healed!*

People do not go to church in order to be healed; they go to church because they have been healed by the grace of God and have resolved to join with the healed in order to heal the world!

In short, one goes to *Jesus Christ* to be healed, and he unites with the *Church* in order to heal others! That notion makes us so nervous that we don't even like to think about it. Yet I am convinced that it is what Jesus thought. Devotion is not for us; it's for the kingdom of God.

Marney's last book, *Priests to Each* Other, is one of the most exciting interpretations of what it means to be a Christian in the modern world that I have ever read. Anyone who reads it cannot help but see that Marney was a deeply spiritual man. But his downfall was that he believed in all truth regardless of who spoke it, and at the same time he believed none of it *completely.* For instance, listen to what he wrote about the church:

We Christians have been given a mighty weapon—the conviction that the man Christ can make us whole, and that men who are being made whole can create a well society aiming to keep the world out and to bring the world in. The Christian church has been a failure at both. We have neither kept the worldliness out nor have we brought the world in. Relevant Christianity . . . demands a new priesthood: a priesthood that believes in the redemption of the world, not the redemption of the church. (11)

Confession and Prayer

- We confess so little so as a result we see so little healing in our lives.

"Confess your sins to each other and pray for each other so that you may be healed. The earnest prayer of a righteous person has great power and produces wonderful results" James 5:16 (LVB).

I am of the conviction there are some Bible principles we access very little. So, we do not see wonderful results.

Relationship and Community

"Do not neglect to meet together, as is the habit of some, but encouraging one another even more as you see the day of the Lord coming nearer." (Hebrews 10:25)

I believe most of our successes will not happen alone. Take a look at the "One Another" scriptures.

The word "kinship" has, for the most part, been lost in today's church culture, but it might not be a bad idea to re-look at this word to see if we can restore a stronger aspect of community (koinonia) into our churches today.

Kinship is defined in dictionaries as "a connection by blood, marriage, or adoption; a family relationship."

Did you know that the New Testament writers share that you and I, as followers of Christ, are called to the concepts of kinship? Actually, the New Testament Greek root word is "allelon", and it is translated as "one another" or "each other." Here are a few of those "one another" texts.

<u>Take a deep breath. Here we go:</u>

- Be at peace with each other." (Mark 9:50)
- "Wash one another's feet." (John 13:14)
- "Love one another" (John 13:34, 35; 15:12, 17; Romans 13:8; 1 John 3: 11, 23; 4: 7, 11, 12; 2 John 5)
- "Be devoted to one another in brotherly love" (Romans 12:10)
- "Honor one another above yourselves." (Romans 12:10)
- "Live in harmony with one another" (Romans 12:16) "
- Stop passing judgment on one another." (Romans 14:13)
- "Accept one another, then, just as Christ accepted you" (Romans 15:7)
- "Instruct one another." (Romans 15:14)
- "Greet one another with a holy kiss" (Romans 16:16; 1 Corinthians 16:20; 2 Corinthians 13: 12)
- "When you come together to eat, wait for each other." (1 Corinthians 11:33)
- "Have equal concern for each other." (1 Corinthians 12:25)
- "Serve one another in love." (Galatians 5:13)
- "Carry each other's burdens" (Galatians 6:2)
- "Be patient, bearing with one another in love." (Ephesians 4:2)

- "Be kind and compassionate to one another" (Ephesians 4:32)
- "Forgiving each other" (Ephesians 4:32; Colossians 3:13)
- "Speak to one another with psalms, hymns and spiritual songs." (Ephesians 5:19)
- "Submit to one another out of reverence for Christ." (Ephesians 5:21)
- "In humility consider others better than yourselves." (Philippians 2:3)
- "Do not lie to each other" (Colossians 3:9)
- "Bear with each other" (Colossians 3:13)
- "Teach...[one another]" (Colossians 3:16)
- "Admonish one another (Colossians 3:16)
- "Make your love increase and overflow for each other." (1 Thessalonians 3:12)
- "Encourage each other" (1 Thessalonians 4:18; 5:11; Hebrews 3:13; 10:25)
- "Build each other up" (1 Thessalonians 5:11)
- "Spur one another on toward love and good deeds." (Hebrews 10:24)
- "Do not slander one another." (James 4:11)
- "Don't grumble against each other" (James 5:9)
- "Confess your sins to each other" (James 5:16)
- "Pray for each other." (James 5:16)
- "Love one another deeply, from the heart." (1 Peter 3:8; 4:8)
- "Live in harmony with one another" (1 Peter 3:8)
- "Offer hospitality to one another without grumbling." (1 Peter 4:9)
- "Each one should use whatever gift he has received to serve others" (First Peter 4:10)
- "Clothe yourselves with humility toward one another"(1 Peter 5:5)
- "Greet one another with a kiss of love." (1 Peter 5:14)

> I find nothing in the Bible that says our spiritual growth happens in a vacuum alone with God.

To hear people, say "Yes I am a Christian but I do not fellowship with other Christians or read a Bible". These people should hear the scripture loudly.

Second Corinthians 13:5 **(NKJV) reads:** "⁵ Examine yourselves *as to* whether you are in the faith. Test yourselves. Do you not know yourselves, that Jesus Christ is in you?—unless indeed you are disqualified." In our day we have a lot of disqualified counterfeit Christians.

First John 3:15 says: "We know that we have passed out of death into life, because we love the brethren. He who does not love abides in death." We love the breather (Christians). Those who do not love is dead (not saved).

First John 4:20 says: "If anyone says, "I love God," and yet hates his brother or sister, he is a liar. For the person who does not love his brother or sister whom he has seen cannot love God whom he has not seen." Another counterfeit Christian.

- The clear teaching of the Bible is that when someone is saved his life will most definitely change as he is a "new creation, the old has gone and the new has come" (2 Corinthians 5:17).
- A true, born-again Christian will strive to bring glory and honor to Christ by living a life that is pleasing to God (1 Peter 1:15–16; 4:1–4).
- True saving faith will indeed produce "fruit" in the life of the believer (James 2:17, 26).
- Thus, if there are no works of love in one's life, a careful self-examination is certainly called for. (2 Corinthians 13:5)

QUESTIONS FOR US TO PONDER?

- What might church look like if we started to take these thirty-eight "one-another" commands of the New Testament and started to act upon them, placing them at the top of our "to-do" lists in ministry?
- Where am I failing to follow these commands, allowing other worldly activities to trump these simple instructions to agape (unconditionally love) allelon (one-another)?

If I were to say: "I am spiritual not religious." What does that mean? For me as a Christian to be spiritual means:

'Committing oneself to Christ, people are committing to a lifestyle prescribed by Jesus (NOT the Church), which promises joyful fulfillment! it's about living life to the fullest. This is not a promise for superficial happiness but a promise of a deep sense of actualizing all the glorious potentialities that God intended for each and every person. God's promise is, "You will have an abundant life. You will have meaning in your life. You will be lifted up and be living on higher ground' (John 10:10, paraphrased).

Lack of Understanding the Role of Giving (Money)

The Bible teaches that how we relate to our money goes to the heart of our relationship with God.

I sometimes feel more comfortable if Jesus hadn't said, "Where your treasure is, there your heart will be also" (Matthew 6:21). I'd be more comfortable if he had said, "Where your heart is, there your treasure will be also." But he said what he meant and he meant what he said. Our attitudes toward money and the priority we place on our possessions are matters of the heart; they go to the core of our identity. Because of the soul-level importance of our relationship with money, we need more than information. We need wisdom.

"Happy are those who find wisdom and those who gain understanding. Her profit is better than silver, and her gain better than gold." (Proverbs 3:13-14)

First, Jesus wants your money to work. (See Luke 19:12-26)

Luke 19:13 says:

"...Use this **money to trade** with until I come back" (KJV)
Put this **money to work**,' he said, 'until I come back.' (NIV)
"...He told them, **'Invest this money** until I come back.'.' (ISV)
Do business with this until I return.' (CEB)

Does this sound like Jesus does not want you to earn money and prosper?

Laziness brings poverty; hard work makes one rich. (Proverbs 10:4)

Second, Jesus actually rebuked the man who did not put his money to work. Jesus called him a "wicked servant" (Luke 19: 22-26). But there are warnings concerning money.

Some Warnings Concerning Money

    a) "Do not covet..." Exodus 20:17
    b) Do not love money! Hebrews 13:5

"Keep your lives free from the love of money and be content with what you have..." Hebrews 13:5

Jesus gives us six warnings concerning money:

1) Beware: The Strangler – "...choked by the cares and riches and pleasures of life, and their fruit does not mature" (Matthew 13:22; Mark 4:18-19; Luke 8:14).
2) Beware: The Worrier – Jesus understood that wealth generates anxiety. Jesus urges us not to be anxious about food or clothing (Matthew 6:19-21, 25-33; Luke 12:22-34).
3) Beware: The Blinder – In one of his most stinging parables (The rich man and Lazarus) Jesus shows how the trappings of riches can blind us (Luke 16:19-23).
4) Beware: The Boss – In another parable Jesus informs us that riches not only blind, they also boss (Luke 16:1-9)
5) Beware: The Dammar – Wealth can have a damning effect on our lives. Jesus underscores this point in a story about a rich fool (Luke 12:13-21).
6) Beware: The Curse – "...but woe to you that are rich, for you have received your consolation" (Luke 6:20)

"Stewardship": I believe that everything I am or own belongs to God.

---

1 Timothy 6:17-19 says: "**17** Command those who are rich in this world that they not be conceited, nor trust in uncertain riches, but in the living God, who richly gives us all things to enjoy. **18** Command that they do good, that they be rich in good works, generous, willing to share, **19** and laying up in store for themselves a good foundation for the coming age, so that they may take hold of eternal life.

The BIG Question: What did Jesus say about tithing? Jesus spoke on tithing only three times!

(1) Luke 11:42 Jesus said:

"But woe to you Pharisees! For you tithe mint and rue and every herb, and neglect justice and the love of God. These you ought to have done, without neglecting the others." (ESV)

(2) Matthew 23:23 Jesus said:

"Woe to you, scribes and Pharisees, hypocrites! For you tithe mint and dill and cumin, and have neglected the weightier matters of the law: justice and mercy and faithfulness. These you ought to have done, without neglecting the others." (ESV)

(3) Luke 18:11-14 Jesus said:

[11] The Pharisee stood and prayed thus with himself, God, I thank thee, that I am not as other men *are*, extortioners, unjust, adulterers, or even as this publican. [12] I fast twice in the week, I give tithes of all that I possess. [13] And the publican, standing afar off, would not lift up so much as *his* eyes unto heaven, but smote upon his breast, saying, God be merciful to me a sinner. [14] I tell you, this man went down to his house justified *rather* than the other: for every one that exalteth himself shall be abased; and he that humbleth himself shall be exalted.

Do you understand, this Pharisee was giving at least 33 % of his income.

It's hardly realistic for a Christian today to assume that Jesus implored us to tithe 33%.

   a) We're not born under the Law, and
   b) we live in an economy of grace (Eph. 3:2).

It's absolutely imperative that the relevance of the Torah of Moses is considered. To the Prushim (Hebrew disciples), it was absolutely relevant; to us, it is essentially irrelevant. Christians, whether Jew or Gentile, keep the Law of Christ (Gal. 6:2), not the Law of Moses.

Jesus was born under the law to fulfill the law (Gal. 4:4-5)... He was bound to it in His life and to rebel against it would be to sin. Also note that the point of these versus when read in context was not to promote tithing, but to promote matters of the heart and show hypocrisy on the parts of the Pharisees. When read aloud and in context no-one will point to tithing and say that is the point, it simply is not the emphasis.

Also note that Jesus refers to the practice of tithing in the past tense... he doesn't say "you ought to do" but instead says, "you ought to have done"—a past tense command.

Jesus did not say the New Covenant church should have tithed, He said the Pharisees should have... The simple truth is that under the law not everyone was to tithe, only certain people were (levites, farmers, and those who tended herds or flocks), Pharisees among them. If we are to Tithe now, where are the instructions that everyone is to tithe, and not just the same certain individuals that tithed under the previous law?

Again, Jesus mentions tithing three times (Matt 23:23, Lk 11:42, Lk 18:11-14) and all three times condemns the tither. Jesus says that the actions of these people were not justified (Luke 18:14) why are using them as an example, and the only example, to justify tithing? The truth is, they should never be used as a model for someone who is justified; nor should they be used as a model for tithing. There simply is no justified tithing model in the New Testament.

Wise Words: "GIVING is the thermometer of our worship"

The New Testament nowhere commands, or even recommends, that Christians submit to a legalistic tithe system (O.T. Mosaic Law). Paul states that believers should set aside a portion of their income in order to support the church (1 Corinthians 16:1-2). The New Testament nowhere designates a percentage of income a person should set aside, but only says it is to be "in keeping with income" (1 Corinthians 16:2).

Above all, all offerings should be given with pure motives and an attitude of worship to God and service to the body of Christ. *"Each man should give what he has decided in his heart to give, not reluctantly or under compulsion* (O.T. Mosaic Law), *for God loves a cheerful giver"* (2 Corinthians 9:7). The Old Testament tithe was a command! It can't get any clearer, the Old Testament saints were under compulsion.

John Wesley (1703–1791) believed three principles about money:

>First, Earn all you can.
>Second, Save all you can.
>Third, Give all you can. (12)

Dr. Charles W. Shedd (1915-2004) once said: "The exciting Church is where they give away their money."

Spiritual Warfare, Satan works to keep God's people bound.

This is another biblical truth we do not access enough. We do not put on each piece of the armor of God, so that we might stand firm in the battles of life.

To the degree that you are a person of biblical truth; a person in whom righteousness dwells, who is committed to what's right; a person whose life is dedicated to peace (not peace at any cost, but the peace that's born of God); a person of faith; a person living in the wholeness of salvation; a person who not only knows the Word of God, but also walks it out— to that degree, you are someone who is blocking the strategies of Satan.

"Be strong in the Lord and in his mighty power. Put on *the full armor of God* so that you can take your stand against the devil's schemes. For our struggle is not against flesh and blood, but against the rulers, against the authorities, against the powers of this dark world and against the spiritual forces of evil in the heavenly realms. Therefore put on the full armor of God, so that when the day of evil comes, you may be able to *stand your ground*, and after you have done everything, to stand. Stand firm then, with the **belt of truth** buckled round your waist, with the **breastplate of righteousness** in place, and with your feet fitted with the readiness that comes from the gospel of peace. In addition to all this, take up the **shield of faith**, with which you can extinguish all the flaming arrows of the evil one. Take the **helmet of salvation** and the **sword of the Spirit**, which is the word of God" (Ephesians 6:10-18).

My conviction is, that if you're not putting on the armor of God then the enemy (Satan) ignores you. Why bother with you if you are not in the battle? If you are not in prayer, worship, Bible study and any type of fellowship the enemy is winning.

1. The evil one (Satan) is only too ready to whisper in our ear: "What a wretch you are. You'd better be sure to keep this quiet. No one would understand. If your friends knew, if your pastor knew – can you image what they'd think of you?

> When Satan talks to you about God he always lies. When Satan talks to God about you he sometimes tells the truth. (Warren Weisrbe)

2. The one who has sinned feels rejection. He does not know whether believers will receive him back or not. His guilt and shame keep driving him further from those he desperately needs.
3. Lack of understanding as Christians that we are at war. Satan and his forces are at war with God and his forces. We need Spiritual Power. (13)

THE RESULTS OF UNRESOLVED CONFLICT, THE FAILURE TO PUT OFF THE OLDMAN AND BE TRANSFORMED

1) Spirituality

    a Impure motives (1 Timothy 1:5)
    b Faulty armor (Ephesians 6:10-18)
    c Poor fruit (1 Corinthians 3:12-15)

2) Emotionally

    a). Loss of identity and purpose
    b). Need to perform for approval and acceptance
    c). Repressed, tormenting emotions (frequently unconscious)
    d). Judgemental
    e). Chronic distress, "hot buttons"
    f). Distorted perceptions of people and circumstances

3) **Physically**

- Of two people who are similar, the one bound by emotional stress will get sick.
- In the year following divorce, the divorcee will have an illness rate twelve times greater than that of a married person.
- Doctors in Fort Worth found that cancer often develops twelve to eighteen months after an emotionally stressful situation and that certain traits are typical to one prone to cancer:
- Greater tendency to hold resentment and a marked inability to forgive.
- A tendency toward self-pity.
- A very poor self-image.
- A poor ability to develop and maintain a meaningful long term relationship.
- Broken or surface relationships (need to hide and/or control).
- Continued sin patterns (sin: that which violates our new nature and purpose).
- Demonic access, potential torment and control.

Failure to accept responsibility for sinful reactions to hurts.

- Blaming others (Genesis 3:12-13).
- Lamenting instead of repenting (1 Samuel 4:7).
- Lack of an atmosphere in local churches of love, acceptance, and forgiveness, providing room for trust, sharing and healing.
- As a result, when the Spirit surfaces something for us to deal with, we hide it, suppress it, and ignore it, adding to the potential for spiritual, and physical sickness.
- Reproducing the "performance for acceptance" model of the world.

Dietrich Bonhoeffer said:

"The pious fellowship permits no one to be a sinner. So everybody must conceal his sin from himself and from the fellowship. We dare not be sinners. Many Christians are unthinkably horrified when a real sinner is suddenly discovered among the righteous. So we remain alone with our sin, living in lies and hypocrisy" (14)

<u>Why</u>?

- We think it is the enemy.
- We are afraid of exposure and rejection.
- We do not know what to do with it.

<u>Lack of Resources</u>: Comforted People Able to Comfort Others.

Fellowship in the true sense means *acceptance, identification, and participation* in the suffering of my brother. Therefore, these are the antecedent conditions that open the community to recognize failure, to welcome confession of wrongdoing, to invite repentance, appropriate restitution and the restoration of deeper levels of trust.

The knowing that our friends and colleagues are available when I need confrontation and clarification of limits or boundaries, and acceptance of me as a person when my behavior is approved or disapproved assure me of my place in relationship and my position as a valued member of the circle of caring Christians (2 Corinthians 1:4-6).

Ignorance to what "loving one another" means.

Pastor Jerry Cook says it well:

"Love is commitment and operates independently of what we feel or do not feel. We need to extend this love to everyone who comes into our church: "Brother, I want you to know that I'm committed to you. You'll never knowingly suffer at my hands. I'll never say or do anything, knowingly, to hurt you. I'll always in every circumstance seek to help you and support you. If you're down and I can lift you up, I'll do that. Anything I have that you need, I'll share with you; and if need be, I'll give it to you. No matter what I find out about you and no matter what happens in the future, either good or bad, my commitment to you will never change. And there's nothing you can do about it. You don't have to respond. I love you, and that's what it means." (15)

WHAT IS THE OPPOSITE OF LOVE?

1 Corinthians 13 is the LOVE chapter in the New Testament. What is the opposite of LOVE? No it is not HATE!

<u>1 Corinthians 13: 4-7 reads</u>:

- Love is patient,
- Love is kind.
- Love It does not envy,
- Love it does not boast,
- Love it is not proud,
- Love it does not dishonor others,
- Love it is not self-seeking,
- Love it is not angered,
- Love it keeps no record of wrongs,
- Love does not delight in evil but rejoices with the truth,
- Love it always protects,

- Love always trusts,
- Love always hopes,
- Love always perseveres.

WHAT KEEPS ME FROM FOLLOWING 1 CORINTHIANS 13?

Letting my SELF get in the way! Being impatient, not kind, having envy, boasting. Not being self-seeking..ect.

Look at the list and see if SELF is in the way of you loving? What is the opposite of love? SELF!

Philippians 2:3 reads:

"Do nothing out of selfish ambition or vain conceit. Rather, in humility value others above yourselves,"

THE THERAPY DETOUR

1. Counseling outside of the concept of community can be a detour.
2. One is not otherwise personally or socially related to him; both "doctor" and "patient" deal with one another as roles rather than as persons.
3. The "doctor's" very involvement in the problem labels the trouble as "illness" rather than "blame", so that one feels less responsible.
4. The "doctor" is sure to accept me, for that is his role.
5. The "doctor" solves my problem by virtue of technical competence and not through personal commitment.
6. The "doctor" serves me for payment. Once payment is made there is no more hold on me and I need fool no debt of commitment to the person or gratitude.
7. I can trust the "doctor" to keep my problem confidential.

As a Christian Counselor, I struggle with the concept of mental illness, because it comes from a medical model which denies God, and true guilt. It enables people to hide in acceptable sickness while denying the power of healing and hope for change through repentance and forgiveness.

ASPECTS OF HUMAN LIFE (Adapted from Lawrence Richards)

HUMAN ISSUE	INDIVIDUAL ASPECT	CORPORATE ASPECT
Identity	Personal Responsibility	Accountability
Intimacy	Individual Worship	Corporate Worship
Sinfulness	Confession	Forgiveness
Lordship	Choice	Freedom
Mortality	Suffering	Compassion
Holiness	Personal Morality	Doing Justice
Commitment	Discipleship	Servanthood (16)

PROBLEM EXPOSURE AND THE PROCESS OF FREEDOM: REPENTANCE

God's heart to restore us includes His exposing conflict and sin in our lives.

   a) The Word of God (2 Timothy 3:16)
   b) Reading / studying / meditating
   c) Teaching / preaching
   d) Books (Bibliotherapy: involves the reading of specific texts with the purpose of healing. It uses an individual's relationship to the content of books and <u>poetry</u> and other written words)
   e) "Hot buttons"
   f) Old memories (songs, places, smells, etc.)
   g) Over reactions (anger, outbursts, etc.)
   h) Relational conflict
   i) Marriage / family (one of the purposes of marriage)

j) Friendships
k) Work related
l) Power encounters û the Holy Spirit confronting us in any context. From our conscience to words of knowledge to major physical responses.
m) Sin symptoms, chronic bondages.

HEALING BEGINS BY TAKING RESPONSIBILITY

Do you wish to get well?" Jesus asks (John 5:6).

"And there remained among the sons of Isreal seven tribes who had not divided their inheritance. So Joshua said to the sons of Israel, How long will you put off entering to take possession of the land which the Lord, the God of your fathers, has given you?" (Joshua 18:2-3)

Why would Jesus ask "Do you wish to get well?"

1) Some people find identity in sickness.
2) Some people do not really want to repent, losing the excuse for their sinful behavior and misery (Rebellion).
3) Some people believe that present misery is deserved payment for past sins, rather than accepting God's forgiveness and forgiving themselves (Ignorance).
4) Sometimes it is easier to cling to emotional wounds, whether they are deserved (the consequences of past sins) or undeserved, than face the feelings that are the result of wounding experiences (Fear).
5) Some people want to put responsivity for their wholeness on others (see Section IV. The Therapy Detour).
6) Some people have been bound for so long, they only talk about freedom (thinking they are fulfilling their responsibility by talking).

TOOLS FOR HEALING (HOW GOD SPEAKS TO US)

a) God speaks through what He has MADE (Psalms 19:1-4; Job 36:26-33; Romans 1:19-20).
b) The BLOOD of Jesus Christ (Hebrews 10:19-22), if you have accepted Him as Lord.
c) God speaks to us through the BIBLE (Colossians 3:16; 2 Timothy 3:16-17; Psalms 43:3; 19:105,133; Proverbs 6:20-23; Hebrews 4:12).
d) By the HOLY SPIRIT within us (John 14:26; 16:13; Psalms 143:10; Acts 8:27-29; 11:12; 16:6-7; 20:22-23; Romans 8:14, 26-27; Romans 9:1).
e) The Holy Spirit speaks through the "fruits of the Spirit" you bear (Galatians 5:22-23)
f) Through PRAYER (James 4:6; 1 Thessalonians 5:17; Philippians 4:6; Ephesians 6:18; Luke 18:1).
g) Your love and MATURITY (Galatians 6:1).
h) The DISCIPLINE of God (Hebrews 12:6-8).
i) The PEACE of God in your heart (Colossians 3:15).
j) The Holy Spirit, and His gifts (John 14:12-14; Romans 1:11; 12:6; 1 Corinthians 12:1-12; 12:27-31; 14:3, 12, 26-30; Ephesians 4:8-14; 1 Timothy 1:6).
k) By the COUNSEL and advice of others (Proverbs 11:14; 12:15; 20:18; 24:6; 1 Corinthians 12:8).

WHY JESUS DIDN'T NEED HEALING: THE KEY TO WHOLENESS

a) Hurts are really bitter attitudes kept alive by our unwillingness to repent and forgive from the heart.
b) Forgiveness as a lifestyle, and trust in God to keep us healthy.
c) Jesus could have needed healing more than anyone:

1. Not accepted, but rejected (John 1:11 and Isaiah 53:3)
2. Probably lost his father while a teenager
3. Identified as an illegitimate child
4. Born in a stable
5. Misunderstood
6. Treated as a criminal
7. "Raped" on the cross

He (Jesus) did not need healing because he never reacted sinfully to what was done to him.

He was tempted to sin by holding un-forgiveness and anger in reaction to hurts (Hebrew 2:17-18).

But even on the cross, he spoke forgiveness to his tormentors, giving us a dramatic picture of his lifestyle of loving (versus sinful) responses (Luke 23:34).

    a) While forgiving, he walked in faith.

"... and while being reviled, he did not revile in return; while suffering he uttered no threats, but kept entrusting himself to Him (God) who judges righteously" (1 Peter 2:23).

I believe Inner healing is twentieth century terminology for biblical sanctification: becoming like Jesus, having a *pure heart, a good conscience,* and *a sincere faith (1* Timothy 1:5).

1. The goal of our instruction is love
2. Pure heart
3. Good conscience
4. Sincere faith

FORGIVENESS FROM THE HEART, FREEDOM FROM THE TORMENTORS

- Ephesians 4:25-31 reads: **²⁵** Therefore, having put away falsehood, let each one of you speak the truth with his neighbor, for we are members one of another. **²⁶** Be angry and do not sin; do not let the sun go down on your anger, **²⁷** and give no opportunity to the devil. **²⁸** Let the thief no longer steal, but rather let him labor, doing honest work with his own hands, so that he may have something to share with anyone in need. **²⁹** Let no corrupting talk come out of your mouths, but only such as is good for building up, as fits the occasion, that it may give grace to those who hear. **³⁰** And do not grieve the Holy Spirit of God, by whom you were sealed for the day of redemption. **³¹** Let all bitterness and wrath and anger and clamor and slander be put away from you, along with all malice.
- 1 Peter 2:1-5 reads: So put away all malice and all deceit and hypocrisy and envy and all slander. **²** Like newborn infants, long for the pure spiritual milk, that by it you may grow up into salvation— **³** if indeed you have tasted that the Lord is good. **⁴** As you come to him, a living stone rejected by men but in the sight of God chosen and precious, **⁵** you yourselves like living stones are being built up as a spiritual house, to be a holy priesthood, to offer spiritual sacrifices acceptable to God through Jesus Christ.
- Matthew 18:21-35 reads: **²¹** Then Peter came up and said to him, "Lord, how often will my brother sin against me, and I forgive him? As many as seven times?" **²²** Jesus said to him, "I do not say to you seven times, but seventy-seven times. **²³** "Therefore the kingdom of heaven may be compared to a king who wished to settle accounts with his servants.[a] **²⁴** When he began to settle, one was

brought to him who owed him ten thousand talents.[b] 25 And since he could not pay, his master ordered him to be sold, with his wife and children and all that he had, and payment to be made. 26 So the servant[c] fell on his knees, imploring him, 'Have patience with me, and I will pay you everything.' 27 And out of pity for him, the master of that servant released him and forgave him the debt. 28 But when that same servant went out, he found one of his fellow servants who owed him a hundred denarii,[d] and seizing him, he began to choke him, saying, 'Pay what you owe.' 29 So his fellow servant fell down and pleaded with him, 'Have patience with me, and I will pay you.' 30 He refused and went and put him in prison until he should pay the debt. 31 When his fellow servants saw what had taken place, they were greatly distressed, and they went and reported to their master all that had taken place. 32 Then his master summoned him and said to him, 'You wicked servant! I forgave you all that debt because you pleaded with me. 33 And should not you have had mercy on your fellow servant, as I had mercy on you?' 34 And in anger his master delivered him to the jailers,[e] until he should pay all his debt. 35 So also my heavenly Father will do to every one of you, if you do not forgive your brother from your heart."

- If hurts are really bitter attitudes kept alive by our unwillingness to repent and forgive from the heart, then for someone to say, "I'm hurt" is really to say, "I'm bitter and unforgiving!"
- As our hearts become impure, we begin to see everything through the lenses of sin (un-forgiveness, anger, etc.).
- In marriage, for example, we find ourselves reacting (over-reacting) to wives and husbands and even children due to unresolved conflict (hurt) from our own mothers and fathers.

For example, we may want our children (especially the first child) to be perfect so we can get the approval of a parent who never gave it in our own childhood, and who may even have died! Yet our need for their approval never died.

We suppress our hurts and resultant feelings (in order to deal with them at an appropriate time in an appropriate way), but never really adequately deal with them.

We then repress those hurts and feelings, lose touch with them, and then hold them unresolved. It is sin to hold unforgiveness, to not forgive from the heart. It separates us from God, binds us in bitterness to the person who has hurt us, and produces symptoms of all kinds, including physical sickness. (2 Samuel 6:20-23).

Until our hearts are purified through accepting responsibility for our sin and sinful reactions, and through forgiving those who hurt us, our motives will be impure, coloring everything we do, and the choices we make.

THE STEPS OF FORGIVENESS (ALONE AND/OR WITH SOMEONE)

    a. Realize that <u>time plus effort</u> are involved

The first step toward the healing process is to recognize that there are no quick cures.

    b. <u>Desire to be healed</u>

Why would someone not want to be healed?

- It could be because of the benefits found in being afflicted (Section: Healing Begins By Taking Responsibility).
- Some believe that present misery is deserved payment.

c. Allow <u>Jesus to help</u> in the healing.

"He was despised and rejected by men, a man of sorrows, and familiar with suffering; Like one from whom men hide their faces, He was despised, and we esteemed Him not. Surely He took up our infirmities, and carried our sorrows... But He was pierced for our transgressions, He was crushed for our iniquities; (our sins) the punishment that brought us peace was upon Him, and by His wounds we are healed (Isaiah 53:3-5).

d. <u>Face and release your emotions.</u>

"You find freedom to forgive when you let yourself feel the pain you want to forgive them for... There is no real forgiving unless there is first relentless exposure and honest judgement. When we forgive evil we do not excuse it, we do not tolerate it, we do not smother it. We look the evil full in the face, call it what it is, let its horror shock and stun and enrage us and only then do we forgive it." (16)

e. Ask God to show us what is at the root of our symptoms; where have we been hurt.

f. Confess the symptoms as sin, realizing they are indicators of deeper sin.

Empty out our hearts to God about our feelings toward the person who has hurt us (sometimes it is helpful to speak to that person as if they were there, telling him/her everything we need to, but were never able to).

g. <u>Receiving</u> God's forgiveness.

"Many Christians are handcuffed by regret. By nature, we know that sin has to be paid for. Consequently, some people nurse their regrets and cling to their grief. The reason? They believe that such an attitude is necessary to punish themselves. Unconsciously, they want to pay for their sins." (17)

   h. Jesus Christ has paid for your sins.

   i. Invite the Spirit of the Lord to come and heal those areas of our hearts and memories which have been bound by hurt and unforgiveness, and to fill us (Luke 11:24-26; Ephesians 5:18).

   j. Invite the Lord to be filling the needs we have, so we do not look to others to meet needs only God can meet.

<u>Remember this</u>: The Holy Spirit is not called the *Comforter* for nothing.

   k. Gain <u>God's perspective</u> on you wounds.

An extremely important part of healing is to recognize that God has the ability and desire to take our hurts, failures and turn them to our good and His Glory (Romans 8:28; Psalms 81:16).

   l. <u>Forgive yourself</u>

Two major causes of emotional problems among evangelical Christians:

   1. Failure to receive forgiveness
   2. ailure to give forgiveness (18)

   m. When you forgive yourself, you become both the forgiver and the forgiven.

   n. <u>Forgive others</u>

Forgiveness has two important sides to this coin.

- The first side of the coin has to do with the mercy of forgiveness
- The other side of the coin is accountability

　　o. Where there is no accountability, there probably will not be much recovery.

Forgiving someone does not change the other person. Abusive relationships will not change until the abuser takes full responsibility for the abuse, with no excuses.

　　p. Forgiving others **changes us**.

The Bible is very clear. There is no forgiveness from God unless we freely forgive our brother from the heart (Matthew 6:15).

　　q. Forgiveness has a **higher priority** than worship (Matthew 5:23-24).

　　i. Forgiveness frees us from the past and from our need to try to seek revenge, either actively or mentally.

　　r. Forgiveness is becoming complete when we love and pray for those that have hurt us (Matthew 5:44).

LEADING SOMEONE TO FIND CHRIST (Adapted from David Watson) (19)

　　a. A Story

"When South Vietnam fell to the rule of the Viet Cong, hundreds of people wanted to flee the armies which ravaged the countryside. When some families saw that they could not leave, many mothers gave their babies to men aboard a ship.

Think of it. Mothers committed their children to people they did not know. They did this hoping that their children would be better off being with strangers than suffering starvation, war, and death.

   b. Three facts to this story:

First, the mothers trusted the judgement of those (in this case, strangers) to whom they gave their children. They believed others would do what was best for the children.

Second, there was no possibility of having their children back – the act was final.

Third, what does it mean to commit ourselves to God? Answer: It is the belief that God is well qualified to take care of what we give to Him. Only God, who knows the future and understands the implications of eternity, is a trustworthy Guide to give our life too.

Fourth, Commitment is not based on feelings.

   c. To return to our story of the Vietnamese mothers:

Regardless of how they felt later, the outcome could not be changed. Our commitment to God is based on the One to whom the commitment is made – not on the feelings of the one who makes the commitment". (Romans 8:31)

Plan of Salvation

What do you understand it takes for a person to go to heaven? Consider how the Bible answers this question: It's a matter of FAITH.

F is for FORGIVENESS
> We cannot have eternal life and heaven without God's forgiveness. -Read Ephesians 1:7a

A is for AVAILABLE
> Forgiveness is available. It is- Available for all. -Read John 3: 16 But not automatic. -Read Matthew 7:21a

I is for IMPOSSIBLE
> It is impossible for God to allow sin into heaven. Because of who He is: God is loving and just. His judgment is against sin. -Read James 2:13a Because of who we are: Every person is a sinner. -Read Romans 3:23 But how can a sinful person enter heaven, when God allows no sin?

T is for TURN Turn means to repent.
> Turn from something-sin and self. -Read Luke 13:3b Turn to Someone; trust Christ only. -Read Romans 10:9

H is for HEAVEN
> Heaven is eternal life. Here -Read John 10:10b Hereafter –Read John 14:3 How can a person have God's forgiveness, heaven and eternal life, and Jesus as personal Savior and Lord? By trusting in Christ and asking Him for forgiveness.

Download the free app on Amazon "Sharing your Faith"

Forsaking
All,
I
Trust
Him.

Appendix A
ILLUSTRATION: A BASIC UNDERSTANDING OF PROBLEM DEVELOPMENT:

      DRUG USE   MARRIAGE   SEXULAL SIN
           PROBLEMS
                    DEPRESSION
       FINANCIAL PROBLEMS   **SUPERFICIAL**
SYMPTOMS: NEED TO CONTROL   NO INTIMACY **SIN**
                    WITH GOD   **RESPONSES**
     SICKNESS
              OUTBURSTS OF ANGER
     HOMOSEXUALITY
                 NO FEELINGS

SELF DEFENSES SUPPRESS / REPRESS FEELINGS

                                          FEELINGS WE HOLD (CONSCIOUS/ UNCONSCIOUS AS
UNDERLYING: ANGER   GUILT   **THE RESULT OF**
                     FEAR   **HURT: OUR SINFUL**
                          ANXIETY

SELF DEFENSES SUPPRESS / REPRESS HURTS

	HURT	**HURT THAT**
RESOLVEDED		**OCCUR WHEN OUR**
PROBLEM		**BASIC NEEDS ARE**
		NOT MET – WHEN
		WE ARE VIOLATED

SELF DEFENSES SUPPRESS / REPRESS NEEDS

	security / Who can I trust?	**BASIC NEEDS THAT**
UNMET	identity / Who am I?	**ONLY GOD CAN**
NEEDS	belonging / Who wants me?	**ULTIMATELY**
	Competence / What do I do well?	**MEET**
	purpose / Why am I alive?	

Appendix B
ILLUSTRATION: FROM SEED (INFORMATION) TO FRUIT (REPRODUCTION)

In the west, we plow, then sow. In the East, where the Bible was written, they sow first, then plow God's Word comes to us as a seed. He then works to plow it into our lives until it bears fruit. Tragically, many accept the seed as the end product, not allowing God to work it into their lives. As a result, they have much information, but little salvation – and nothing of life to give away (Philippians 2:2-13).

SOWING

INFORMATION Luke 1:76-77	GENERALLY PASSED ON WITHOUT PERSONAL OWNERSHIP
REVELATION Luke 2:30	THE INFORMATION COMES ALIVE AND MORE RELEVANT

PLOWING

CONVICTION Acts 1:36-37	THE HOLY SPIRIT BRINGS PERSONAL APPLICATION, FREQUENTLY THE PROCESS ENDS HERE SINCE IT FEELS GOOD TO FEEL BAD
CONFESSION / REPENTANCE Luke 19:8	TAKING PERSONAL RESPONSIBILITY FOR SINFUL REATIONS AND CHANGE. THE PRIMARY GOAL OF THE SPIRT THREE ASPECTS OF COMMUNICATION

GROWING

SALVATION Luke 19:9	THE EXPERIENCE OF DELIVERANCE AND FREEDOM
CONTINUED OBEDIENCE 1 Peter 1:14-16	EXPANDS THE DIMENSION OF SALVATION

REPROWDUCING

IMPARTATION 2 Corinthians 1:3-7	THE ABILITY TO GIVE AWAY WHAT IS OWNED, TO COMFORT OTHERS WITH COMFORT (SALVATION) RECEIVED
RELATION John 15:4-8	WE CONTINUE TO BEAR FRUIT ONLY AS WE CONTINUE TO ABIDE AND OBEY

Footnotes

1. Gary Collins; The Biblical Basis of Christian Counseling for People Helpers: Relating the Basic Teachings of Scripture to People's Problems (Pilgrimage Growth Guide) (January 1, 1993)

2. Dr. John White, Putting the Soul; Back into Psychology, When Secular Values Ignore Spiritual Realities, Pg. 64).

3. Paul Tournier, Secrets Hardcover – Pg. 57, 1970

4. Kirwan, William T. Biblical Concepts for Christian Counseling: A Case for Integrating Psychology and Theology by published by Baker Academic (1984) Pg. 63).

5. Crab, Larry, Effective Biblical Counseling: A Model for Helping Caring Christians Become Capable Counselors – Oct 28, 2014

6. Jared C. Wilson and Ray Ortlund, Gospel Wakefulness – Oct 6, 2011 Pg. 69

7. The Transformation of the Inner Man by John Loren Sandford (Bridge Publishing) 1982) Pg. 5

8. James H. McConkey, Three Fold Secret of the Holy Spirit Paperback – June 10, 2015

9. John Piper Desiring God: Meditations of a Christian Hedonist Paperback – April 17, 2003

10. David A. Seamands, Healing for Damaged Emotions – Mar 1, 2015

11. Carlyle Marney, Priests to Each Other, Valley Forge: Judson Press, (1971) Pg. 9

12. James A. Harnish , Earn. Save. Give.: Wesley's Simple Rules for Money – May 5, 2015

13. Christianity with Power: Your Worldview and Your Experience of the Supernatural by Charles H. Kraft (Paperback 1989) Pg. 170

14. Bonhoeffer, Dietrich, Life Together: The Classic Exploration of Faith in Community (Edition 1St Edition) (1978) Pg. 110

15. Love, Acceptance and Forgiveness (Paperback – 1979) by Jerry Cook; Stanley C. Baldwin, (Author) Pg. 13

16. A practical theology of spirituality by Larry Richards (Hardcover – 1987) Pg. 66

17. Forgive and Forget: Healing the Hurts We Don't Deserve (Plus) by Lewis B. Smedes (Paperback, 1984) Pg. 36

18. Failure : The Back Door to Success by Erwin W. Lutzer (Paperback ,1977) Pg. 59

19. Healing for Damaged Emotions by David Seamonds, (Pao\perback, Victor Books 1991) Pg. 29-32

20. Called & Comitted by David Watson (Paperback 1982) Pg. 153-154

www.ingramcontent.com/pod-product-compliance
Lightning Source LLC
Chambersburg PA
CBHW052209110526
44591CB00012B/2139